3Kiddos Publishing
Nose to Nose with Atlas

Distributed In Partnership With
3Kiddos Publishing

www.3kiddospublishing.com

ISBN:
979-8-9898171-7-7

I am Atlas.

My mom is a dog groomer and she gives fun hair cuts on dogs that are big,

small, short, tall or even long !

That means I get to meet so many

new

friends!

Let's get nose to nose with my new friends. Maybe we can find one just like me!

This is
Lambeau
a Shih Tzu.

This is

Goose

a mini Dachshund.

and he:
Can have a long, short or wire coat.

Dachshunds should be 11 pounds or less.

This breed used to hunt badgers!

Dachshunds make a LOUD watch dog.

Just like me.

This is a Yorkshire Terrier.

Clara

and she:
is very tiny - only about 7 pounds.

Yorkshire Terriors have been a rat dog and a lap dog

This breed became an official breed in 1870!!

Clara has beautiful hair that grows past her toes.

Just like me.

This is

Tally

a French Bulldog.

This is Gage an Australian Shepherd.

And he:
Can be 3 main colors.
Black, Chocolate, and Yellow.

He has a thick "otter tail" for swimming.

His breed is one of America's most popular dogs.

Labradors are very food motivated.

Tonka loves treats.

Just like me.

This is

lettie
a
Standard
Poodle.

And she: **is from Germany!**

Poodles have a fancy haircut that protects their joints from cold water.

This breed was used to hunt ducks and geese.

They also have curly hair.

Just like me.

This is *Archie.*

a Maltese.

And she:
was kept in the sleeves of wealthy Roman women

This breed originally comes from Malta

They were also in New York's first Westminster Dog Show!!

Malteses have only had one job- to be a loved pet.

Just like me.

and she:
can be any color from light cream to dark red

This breed is often used to guide the blind.

They came from Scotland!!

Retrievers loves to swim
and play in the water

Just
like
me.

I am *Atlas*
and I...
am a little bit of this
and a little bit of that...

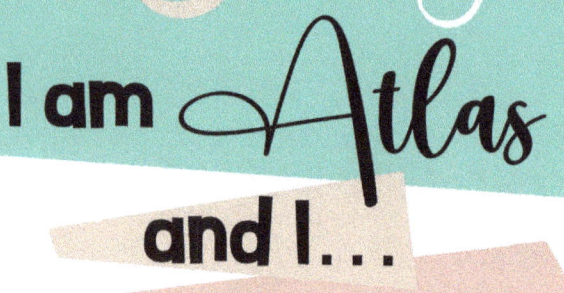

But nose to nose
I know everyone is…

Meet Jami Johnson & Atlas

Jami spends most of her time as a self employed groomer, through a locally (& woman) owned shop **Heart to Heart Pet Salon.**

In between baths and brushes, Jami can be found keeping up with her teenage kids schedules.

This book has been in the back of her mind since they were little.

"I started dog grooming over 8 years ago; this book is a nod to the dog who got me started." (Atlas)! "

Story Salute
2024
winner

www.ingramcontent.com/pod-product-compliance
Lightning Source LLC
Chambersburg PA
CBHW041132120626
46547CB00019B/2958